Endorsements

From Some of My Grands:

"Nana, I like your stories because they teach me about God." – Mary, age 4

"Nana, I think your book is AWESOME! It explained a lot of things to me." –Alice, age 8

"I like how Nana explains it all. I get it!" – Macey, age 9

"I like the story about Rudolph. It teaches you that even though sometimes you're sad, there's always a part to be happy." – Andrew, age 6

"Nana tells great stories!" – Kathryn, age 11

(In answer to the devotional question, What has God given you?) "God has given me joy!"

– Caleb, age 6

From My Daughters:

"As a natural teacher, Mom brings lessons to life, pointing each of our hearts to the true meaning of Christmas." – Alayna

"As a working mom, I struggle with feeling like I have to choose between my own quiet time versus helping my children with theirs…but this devotional fills both needs. Deep truths for me, yet simple revelations for my children=peace for this momma's heart." – Candace

"Sitting together to color and talk about the signs of Christmas is such a natural way to engage my little ones in God's great story." – Courtney

"A fun way to integrate Jesus' signs into all parts of His birthday celebration." –Becca

From My Sons:

"Nana rocks!" – Stuart

"Anything my mom writes about is going to bring healing to one's heart." – Jonathan

"I really like this concept: something for moms, something for kids." – Geoffrey

"This is a wonderful resource for integrating the wonder of the season with the reality of Jesus." – Brandon

Taming the Tinsel:

"Mom-Moments" For Mother & Child

By

Johnnita H. Cook

Coloring Pages by

Johnnita Cook

Scripture quotations taken from the New American Standard Bible® (NASB), Copyright © 1960, 1962, 1963, 1968, 1971, 1972, 1973, 1975, 1977, 1995 by The Lockman Foundation Used by permission. www.Lockman.org
Exceptions to NASB are noted within the text and include
The ESV® Bible (The Holy Bible, English Standard Version®), copyright © 2001 by Crossway, a publishing ministry of Good News Publishers. Used by permission. All rights reserved.
KJV—the King James Version, public domain.
NIV The Holy Bible, New International Version®. Copyright© 1973, 1978, 1984, 2011 by Biblica, Inc.™. Used by permission of Zondervan
The NLT The Holy Bible, NEW LIVING TRANSLATION, Copyright© 1996, 2004, 2007 by Tyndale House Foundation. Used by permission of Tyndale House Publishers, Inc., Carol Stream, Illinois 60188. All rights reserved. Used by permission.
TLB- The Living Bible copyright© 1971. Used by permission of Tyndale House Publishers, Inc., Carol Stream, Illinois 60188. All rights reserved.
TPT-The Passion Translation®. Copyright © 2017, 2018 by Passion & Fire Ministries, Inc. Used by permission. All rights reserved. ThePassionTranslation.com

Cover photo by Jeswin Thomas on Upsplash.com
Author photo & family photo by Alan Cook
Cover design by Janis Teller. Contact at Chelsea2583@hotmail.com
ISBN 978 1 73284200 7

Dedication

To my four wonderful daughters who daily disciple their children to love the Lord.
To my "grands" who are, of course, "the best"! (Spoken like a true grandma.)

Table of Contents

Introduction

Christmas is coming and so is the frenzy. The mall pitches its wares as our social calendars snap into overdrive. Pretty soon we're tempted to beg, "Please, oh, please! Could I just skip December?" But how do we skip the school pageant or the office party? The decorating, baking, and buying gifts? Every December 26th, we vow, "Next year I'm going to Tame the Tinsel. I'm going to keep my family focused on the Christ Child. Sadly, if your life is anything like mine was as a young mother, when next year comes, frenzy hits "replay."

All of us want to keep our hearts anchored to Jesus amidst the chaos. We all need Mom-Moments for ourselves and with our children. On each page of this Christmas devotional are reflections for mom and mini-lessons for the children. There are children's verses, intended to plant the word of God in their hearts. They just might like to learn them with you. The coloring pages are to reinforce the messages they have heard.

God has graciously "snuck" spiritual symbols into the secular culture around us. In many ways, the nativity of His Son is hidden in plain sight. For example, candy canes remind us of Jesus, the Good Shepherd. Christmas bells call our hearts to worship. Flashing lights and soft candles symbolize Jesus, the light of the world. Each time we see a symbol, it's a chance to turn our eyes upon Jesus in thanks and worship. Your children might like to play an ongoing game during Advent, to see just how many symbols they can spot.

As we open the eyes of our children's hearts to the symbols of Advent, we teach them to apply the revelation of Romans 1:20. God says that through the created world He shows us His unseen powers and His divine nature. In this Advent season, we can use familiar symbols to whisper God's faithfulness in sending His Son. Taming the Tinsel is no easy task, with all the distractions around us. Yet we believe the truth of His promise:

You will keep in perfect peace…all whose thoughts are fixed on you! (Isaiah 26:3)

December 1: The Coming of Messiah

Moment For Mom:

"How much longer, Mommy?" We have all heard that question a thousand times and probably will a thousand more. Children know that when Christmas comes, it's time for presents! And it is so hard to wait.

Now, waiting for Christ's coming is not at all new. From ancient days, God's people awaited the promised Messiah. Their hearts yearned for Him, but most died before He came. Simeon and Anna had waited for Jesus all their lives and rejoiced exceedingly to see Him with their own eyes (Luke 2:21-38).

Sometimes I wonder if we fully appreciate the privilege of living in the age when Christ has already come. Ours is the full revelation of how Jesus came to ransom men from their sin. His life on earth, as seen in Scripture, is a picture to us of what the Father is really like (John 14:9). It is also a pattern for how we are to live, from day to day.

In this age, our waiting is not for the initial coming of Christ, but for His glorious return. In the meantime, God dwells with us "to purify for Himself a people for His own possession, zealous for good deeds" (Titus 2:14). We can live in His strength, as we invite Him to live in us. He is Immanuel, "God with us."

Moment With My Child:

Sometimes it's hard to wait for Christmas, especially when there are presents under the tree with *your* name on them! What do you think they might be? Hey, you might like to hear Alvin and the Chipmunks sing their own song about waiting for Christmas. (Link: https://www.youtube.com/watch?v=mDtOwSjIDFw)I'll bet you know just how the Chipmunks feel. Of course, we are not the only ones who have waited for Christmas. For a very long time before Jesus came, people waited and waited for Him to be born. Because Jesus came to earth that first Christmas Day, people can now live with Him all the time. How do we do that? By asking Jesus into our hearts.

They will call him Immanuel, which means "God is with us." Matthew 1:23 NLT

Mom note: Look! The clock is waiting for Christmas too.

December 2: Silent Night

The song "Silent Night" speaks of the "heavenly peace" which Christ ushered into the world. Since the fall of Adam, there has been no peace between God and man, only the chasm which separates God's holiness from man's sinfulness. Jesus, the Second Adam, came to re-connect us with the Father. Only through Jesus can we enjoy peace with God.

"Silent Night" has been translated into over three hundred languages. Perhaps that is because of its universal theme. All of us want the peace of heart and mind which comes with Jesus. To quote the hymn's lyrics, the "Son of God, love's pure light" came as "Christ the Savior." He came with "redeeming light," showing us the way to heaven. By accepting Christ's death on the cross for the forgiveness of our sins, we can be sure that we will spend eternity with Him. Thus heavenly peace can live in our hearts.

Jesus bought our eternal peace on the cross. Our job is to seek daily peace, even when life is chaotic. We do that by communing with God: listening to Him speak through His word, talking with Him, and lifting our hearts to Him in the "dailies" of life. John 17:3 says that eternal life begins now, as we get to know God personally. It's not just head-knowledge that gives us peace. It's getting to know God's heart, as He speaks to our souls.

Moment With My Child:

It was a cold, snowy Christmas Eve many, many years ago. The pastor of a village church was sad. The next day was Christmas, and the people would want to sing, but the church's organ had broken. Suddenly the pastor remembered a poem he had written, and he asked a guitar player to write a simple tune to go with it. The song "Silent Night" was born that very day. The song talks about "heavenly peace." Peace is what you feel when you go to sleep hugging your (insert name of favorite toy). Or when you are frightened and your parents say, "It's okay." Peace is feeling safe because you know that Jesus loves you. When Jesus was born, He brought us peace.

His name will be called...Prince of Peace. Isaiah 9:6

December 3: Christmas Wreaths

Moment For Mom:

Even a geometry whiz can't find the beginning of a circle. A circle has no beginning, just as it has no end. God's love is like that. He loved us before the world began, and He loves us still. Christmas wreaths are usually circular, a perfect symbol for the never-ending love of God, which caused Him to send Jesus. He promises to never, ever forsake us (Matthew 28:20).

God's love is not like human love. All of us have experienced the heartbreak which can come at the hands of others. Disloyalty, betrayal, even abandonment are human arrows which pierce the heart. Even the circle of a wedding band, professing endless love, can be severed. But the love of God cannot. In fact, He brings His divine love near to heal the brokenhearted and bind up all their wounds (Psalm 147:3).

In the Bible, God promises to step into every human relationship where we have experienced grief. God calls Himself our father and husband. Jesus is the groom, the friend, and the brother. The Holy Spirit comes to us as comforter, counselor, and guide. Our fellowship with them, on earth and in heaven, will literally never end. God, thank You for Your love and Your faithfulness. I can trust You, knowing that Your love for me will never end. You will love me, love me, love me, no matter what. Even when I find it hard to love myself.

Moment With My Child:

What shape is a Christmas wreath? That's right. A circle. Can you point to where it begins and ends? No, you can't. Why? Because the circle has no beginning and no end. It keeps going and going. God's love is like that. He always loved you, and He always will. Holly is often used in Christmas wreaths. The holly is an evergreen plant. Its green color is always there. Like the greenness of the holly, Jesus says that He will always be with us. He will never, ever leave us. The red berries of the holly remind us of the blood that Jesus shed on the cross. He died to pay for our sins. Each time you see a Christmas wreath, remember Jesus' love for you is never ending just like a circle.

The Lord's loving-kindness never ceases. Lamentations 3:22

December 4: Christmas Trees

Moment For Mom:

Back in the 1960s, aluminum Christmas trees were all the rage. They came in many colors, with a lighted, revolving color fan to accent their glow. They were dubbed "evergleams" and were quite the sight. But in replacing "evergreens," they supplanted a rich heritage.

Bringing evergreen trees inside dates back centuries. One story is that Boniface, a missionary to Germany, came across a group of pagans one Christmas Eve, preparing to sacrifice a human to their god Thor. The ritual was taking place beneath the god's Thunder Oak. With great boldness, Boniface felled the oak and then pulled up a small fir tree nearby. He instructed the people to take fir trees into their homes, as the centerpiece of the evening's celebration. He showed them that the trees pointed upward to the true God. The ever-green foliage represented the never-ending life they could have with Him. There was no need for human sacrifice, Boniface told them. Jesus had already died for them.

Most of us have collected ornaments over the years, celebrating important events in our lives. They are like memorial stones in the Bible, reminding us of God's faithfulness. Trimming the tree is a perfect time to reflect on God's continual goodness to us and to thank Him for it.

Moment With My Child:

Why do you think we have trees *inside* our houses at Christmas? One story is that a missionary named Boniface told the people to bring them inside. (Missionaries are people who go to different places to tell others about Jesus.) Boniface showed the people how Christmas trees point to heaven, where God lives. The lights on the tree remind us of Jesus, who calls Himself the light of the world. The ornaments remind us of the good times we've had over the years. Christmas is a wonderful time to thank God for being so good to us.

Jesus…is the true God and eternal life. I John 5:20

Mom note: While talking with your children about the special tree in your house, you could share the legend of the three trees. LINK: https://www.youtube.com/watch?v=DjlOViJlM3U Each tree started out with a vision of how it wanted to be used. In the end, they were all used in the life of Jesus. He uses us all for His glory.

December 5: The Lowly Donkey

Moment For Mom:

I was on vacation in the Caribbean when a donkey broke loose from his owner and ran straight toward me. "Benji!" yelled its master, as the donkey stopped short and nuzzled my side. "Benji! What are you doing?" Now, I was not at all upset by Benji's affection. God had just used him to show me something marvelous. I saw that all the way down Benji's back was a stripe of dark, upright hair, crossed by an identical stripe on his shoulders. Together the lines made a perfect symbol of Christ's cross. Of all His animals, God chose to honor the donkey with an emblem of His Son. Perhaps it's because a donkey would bear Mary to Bethlehem and the triumphant King Jesus into Jerusalem.

It's not unusual to hear donkeys demeaned as stupid beasts of burden. But being a burden-bearer is not always a bad thing. In fact, it can be life-saving. Jesus bore the sins of the world. He took on Himself a load that none of us could carry.

People may judge us as they do the donkey, by our appearance, power, or wealth. God is not like that. He judges our willingness to carry the mark of Jesus in our hearts and in our lives.

Moment With My Child:

In Italy, children sing about Dominick the Christmas Donkey. Dominick carries Santa's toys for him because they are too heavy for the reindeer. Can you think of another donkey who carried something precious at Christmas? That's right! When it was time for Jesus to be born, a donkey carried Mary, Jesus' mother, to Bethlehem. Maybe that's why God lets donkeys wear a special sign of His Son. Down the donkey's back is a stripe of dark hair, crossed by an identical stripe on its shoulders. Together they form a picture of the cross that Jesus bore. Now, we don't have hair on our backs or shoulders, but we can carry the invisible cross of Jesus in our hearts. It comes out in our kind words and actions. Others may judge us by how we look on the outside, but God looks at our heart.

The Lord looks at the heart. I Samuel 16:7

December 6: Christmas Colors

Moment For Mom:

I was out last December with a toddler grandchild when she tugged on my arm and pointed, "Look, Nana! Christmas colors!" During December, the world turns red and green, with gold and white for good measure. One day it struck me how closely those colors parallel the ones of the Wordless Book. Now, you may or may not be familiar with that little teaching aid. My children and their friends learned the good news of the gospel from a pamphlet with nothing but colors. It worked. Charles Spurgeon used it to preach, as did D.L. Moody and beloved hymn-writer Fanny Crosby. This is the message it preached:

RED stands for the blood of Jesus, shed that we might have eternal life. The Bible says that without the shedding of blood, there is no forgiveness of sin (Hebrews 9:22).

GREEN is the color of growth. God gives us strength to grow in Him, that He might transform us from glory to glory (II Corinthians 3:18).

GOLD is the color of the King, and we are the King's children (Galatians 3:26). Heaven itself is made of pure gold (Revelation 20:18).

WHITE is the color of purity: the pure heart of Jesus when He died for our sins (Hebrews 7:26). The blood of Jesus washes our hearts as white as snow.

Moment With My Child:

When you think of Christmas, what colors do you see? That's right: red and green. Of course, we also see a good bit of gold and white. All the colors look bright and happy on a background of black. Christmas colors explain why Jesus came to earth. How do they do that? The different colors stand for different things. Black is the darkness in our hearts before we know Jesus. Red is the color of blood that Jesus shed. White is how our hearts look when the blood of Jesus washes our sins away. Gold is the color of heaven. Green is the color of growth. We grow each day by reading our Bible and praying. Let's listen to the song about the Wordless Book. (link: https://www.youtube.com/watch?v=iuWJr9Wq8GY)

Isn't that fun? The colors around us at Christmas tell us the story of Jesus. He came to pay for all our sins: for all the things that we do wrong.

Grow in the grace and knowledge of our Lord and Savior Jesus Christ. II Peter 3:18

WORDLESS GOSPEL

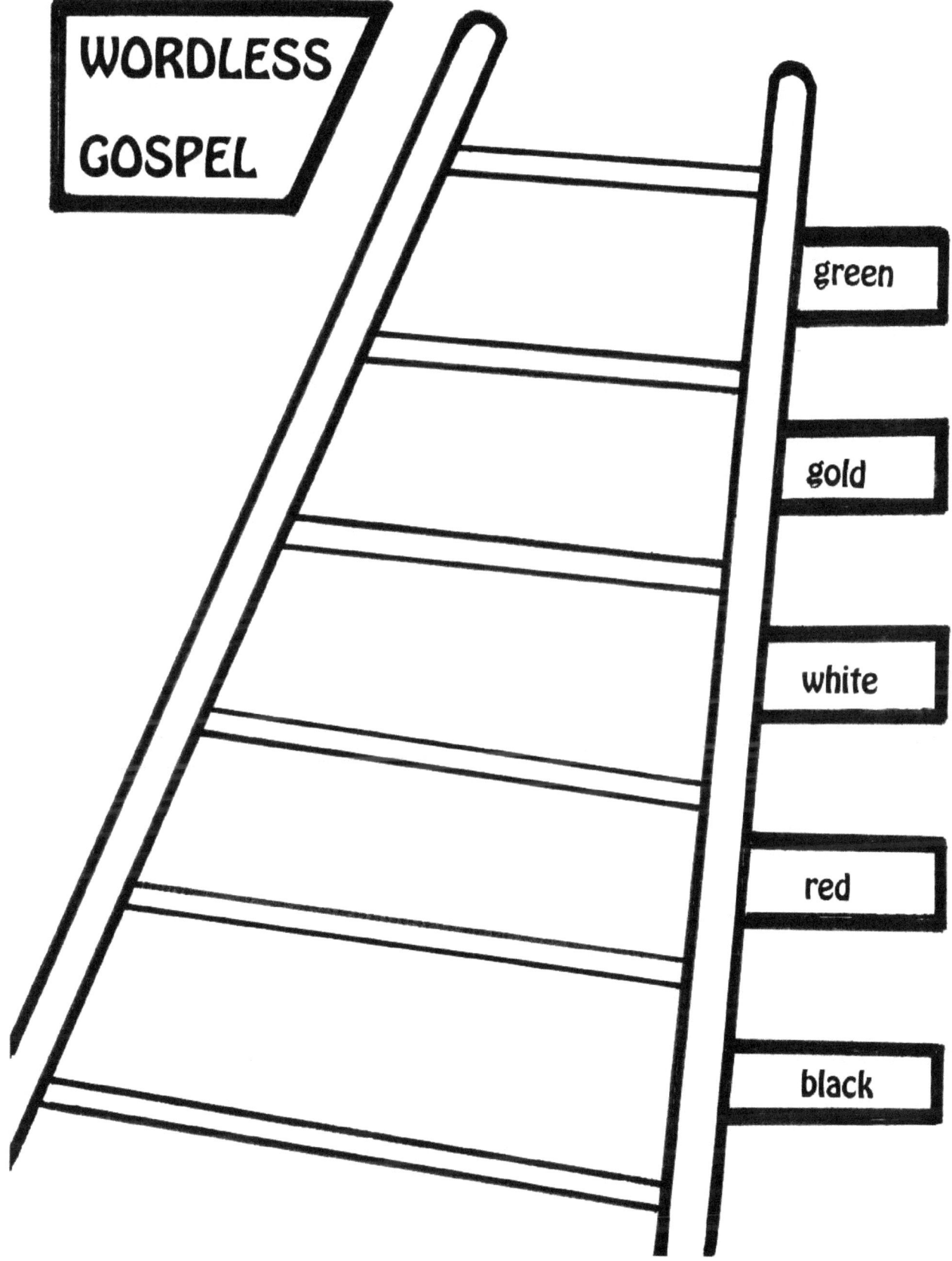

green

gold

white

red

black

December 7: Rudolph the Red-Nosed Reindeer

Moment For Mom:

A friend of mine works in a facility for mentally challenged adults. One Christmas she met Joey, a young man in his twenties, walking down the hall. Tears streamed down Joey's cheeks. "What's the matter, Joey?" she asked him. Back came his tender-hearted reply, "The reindeer were so mean to Rudolph." Chances are Joey had experienced in his life the same pain of differentness that Rudolph had. His mental slowness was his own bright red nose.

My friend was able to share with Joey the end of Rudolph's story: the part where Rudolph became Santa's hero on that foggy Christmas Eve. Because Rudolph's nose could guide the sleigh through the night, little children received the presents Santa had prepared for them.

All of us have red noses of one kind or another. My granddaughter Victoria was born with spina bifida and is confined to a wheelchair. But that doesn't keep her spirit from shining through the darkness. It is a light which guides others to her Savior, to receive the gifts He has prepared for them. Her overcoming attitude points others to Jesus, her strength.

God created each of us with a very special purpose, even if we don't yet know what it is. God knows the end from the beginning, and we do not. He works in our circumstances to accomplish His perfect plan. We may sometimes feel different from those around us, but we are beautiful in His eyes.

Moment With My Child:

Rudolph wanted to be like all the other reindeer, but he was not. Rudolph had a big, red, shiny nose that made all the other reindeer laugh at him and call him names. He was miserable until that night when the fog rolled in, and Santa could not see to deliver his toys. That's when Rudolph became the hero. His bright red nose became the light that led Santa's sleigh through the night. There was a plan for Rudolph all along. He just didn't know it.

Have you ever felt sad like Rudolph did? Have you ever felt different? Remember, God has a plan for your life, too. You are special to Him. And you are special to me.

I know the plans I have for you, declares the Lord. Jeremiah 29:11

December 8: Sweet Treats

Moment For Mom:

You can have the chestnuts roasting on the open fire. I'll take the cookies in the oven every time. Their sweet aroma reminds us of *delicious* Christmases past and of fun times around the mixing bowl. As a bonus, many treats take us deep into the message of Christmas:

GINGERBREAD HOUSES. The spices in gingerbread produce its "earthy" color. It's a reminder that Jesus became man to save us from our sins.

SUGAR COOKIES. As we cut out and decorate shaped cookies, we can tell the Christmas story again and again: the star of Bethlehem, the gift of Jesus, wreaths of God's eternal love, candy canes of the Good Shepherd's care.

BIRTHDAY CAKE FOR JESUS: Children look forward to their own birthdays, so they love to celebrate the birthday of Jesus. Try topping the icing with symbolic Christmas candy: Lifesavers, because He saves us from our sins; Rolos, as crowns for the King; gold coins for the many treasures He brings.

God refers to His Word as "sweet" (Psalm 119:103). Likewise there is the sweetness of His presence, which makes the bitterness of our lives once again sweet (Exodus 15:33-36). The sweet (kind) words we speak to others can encourage them during the stressful Christmas season. They can bring the taste of God's goodness into others' lives.

Moment With My Child:

On Christmas we celebrate Jesus' birthday! What do you like about *your* birthday? Balloons? Cake and ice cream? Presents? Playing games? It's fun to celebrate the special day that God gave YOU to our family. God also loves for us to celebrate the day that He gave His Son to the world. Happy Birthday, Baby Jesus! Hey, do you like to eat Christmas cookies? Of course you do! Why? Because they are so sweet. Jesus is just a sweet to our hearts as cookies are to our taste. Our hearts don't have mouths, of course! But having Jesus live in our hearts is a very sweet thing. When we enjoy sweet Christmas treats, we remember the sweetness of Jesus.

O taste and see that the Lord is good. Psalm 34:8

December 9: Poinsettias

Moment For Mom:

My father was a florist, and when I was young I helped in his shop. At Christmas, my job was to water the sea of poinsettias that covered the floor. Everyone wanted poinsettias, the flower of the season.

Most poinsettias are red, but they also come in white and pink. Red reminds us of the blood that Jesus would one day shed on the cross. White is the purity of Christ's sinless heart. Pink is the universal color of love. Because of His love for us, Jesus came to the world to suffer and die, to pay for our sins. He sacrificed Himself to cleanse us and make us whole. The leaves of the poinsettia produce purple dye, the color of royalty. Its sap is used for physical healing. The poinsettia is a fitting symbol for the kingly healer of our spirit, soul, and body.

The legend of the poinsettia tells of a young girl who picked wildflowers for the Christ Child, to leave at the crèche in her church. As soon as she placed them before the manger, God transformed them into beautiful poinsettias. God is still in the transformation business, changing us from "weeds" into the image of His Son (II Corinthians 3:18). The poinsettia is a flower glorious in its beauty. But it is nothing, compared to the marvelous changes God generates in His children. It is nothing compared to the beauty of God.

Moment With My Child:

Do you like to pick flowers for people? Of course you do. It's a sign that you love them. Red Christmas flowers are called poinsettias. Their leaves are shaped like the star of Bethlehem, and the prickly flowers in the middle are like the crown of thorns that Jesus wore. The legend of the poinsettia says that once a little girl picked weeds as a gift for Jesus, to place in the nativity scene at her church. When she set them before the manger, God changed them into beautiful poinsettias. When we worship and obey Jesus, He makes our hearts beautiful, just like the poinsettia.

He has made everything beautiful in its time. Ecclesiastes 3:11 NIV

December 10: Christmas Bells

Henry Wadsworth Longfellow wrote "I Heard the Bells on Christmas Day" during the bloody Civil War. He asked how there could be peace on earth, with his countrymen killing each other. His own heart had little peace, as he grieved his son's wounding in the war and the death of his wife in a tragic fire. As Longfellow wrote, God strengthened his heart to see the bigger picture. When Jesus comes into our lives, He brings peace, regardless of the turmoil around us:

When men repent and turn from sin, the Prince of Peace then enters in.

And grace imparts within their hearts, His peace on earth, good will to men.

There's something about bell-ringing that resonates deep within us, quickening our hearts to the season: the peace of hand bells, the generosity of "red bucket" bells, and the joy of jingle bells. My favorite bells are the jingling ones, not just because they please my "child within," but because they remind me of their significance in Jesus' day. There were jingling bells on the hem of the high priest's garment when he entered the Holy of Holies, seeking God's forgiveness for the people's sins. Jesus came as our Great High Priest, effecting forever a peace with God that men might enter in.

MOMENT WITH MY CHILD:

When Christmas comes, church bells ring, calling us to praise the newborn king. Other bells ring by the red buckets you sometimes see when we are shopping. They call us to put money in the bucket for people in need. Choirs sometimes play hand bells, ringing out our favorite Christmas songs. I'll bet one of your favorites is "Jingle Bells." Mine, too. The jingling bells remind me of the bells on the high priest's robe in Jesus' day. The people could hear when the high priest went before God to ask forgiveness for their sins. Jesus came as the Great High Priest, so that God could be our best friend forever. When we hear Christmas bells jingle, it is a time to remember all that Jesus did for us as our Great High Priest.

We have a great high priest...Jesus the Son of God. Hebrews 4:14

December 11: Candy Canes

Candy canes were the brainchild of the choir master at Cologne Cathedral, hundreds of years ago. He doled out hard candy sticks to young children, to keep them from disrupting his Christmas performance. Later the sticks were adapted to the candy cane we know today. Its hardness represents the rock-solid foundation we have through faith in Jesus Christ. But just as Jesus offered His body to be broken, so the candy cane can be broken…crushed.

Jesus predicted His death at the Last Supper, when He told His disciples, "This is my body, which is broken for you" (I Corinthians 11:24 KJV). We respond to His brokenness by submitting ourselves to Him, in repentance for our sins. This involves the brokenness of our pride, as well as the surrender of our wills.

Contrary to present cultural thought, the world does not revolve around each of us. God is God and we are not. We are precious to Him, but designed to be dependent on His goodness. Self-sufficiency is not a part of the equation. King David learned, in repenting for his sinful fall, that "the sacrifices of God are a broken spirit; A broken and a contrite heart, O God, You will not despise" (Psalm 51:17). The fresh, peppermint flavor of the candy cane is like hyssop, often used in the Bible for cleansing. When we invite Jesus into the brokenness of our hearts, He cleanses us from sin. We can feel the "freshness" of His forgiveness inside our hearts.

MOMENT WITH MY CHILD:

Candy canes are yummy, and they also remind us of Jesus. The white stripes say that Jesus never sinned. His heart is as white as snow. The red stripes stand for the blood He shed to pay for our sins. The shape of the candy cane is like the Good Shepherd's crook. A shepherd keeps his sheep safe by putting the crook around them and drawing them back from danger. Jesus protects us from the attacks of the Devil. When you turn the cane upside down, what letter do you see? That's right. It's a "J" for "Jesus."

The blood of Jesus…cleanses us from all sin. I John 1:7

December 12: Christmas Fruit

Moment For Mom:

Fruitcakes get a bum rap. Even if one baked in 1898 withstood a World War II bombing—which it did—that's no reason to disrespect them. After all, fruit is important to God's kingdom. Jesus was called the fruit of Mary's womb. Man is the ultimate fruit of God's creation. Then, too, there are the fruits of the Spirit: love, joy, peace, longsuffering, gentleness, goodness, meekness, temperance, and faith. God told the human race to be fruitful and multiply. Jesus exhorted the people to be fruitful with their talents, multiplying the gifts that God gave them.

In John 15, Jesus tells the parable of the vine and the branches. He is the vine, and we are the branches. When we abide in Him, we bear much fruit. On the cross, Jesus made possible the fruit of righteousness in our lives. Our job is to receive that fruit and to share His message with others. As mothers, we are bringing forth our children as fruit in God's kingdom. It's not a whirlwind production, but more like a twenty-year project. Each day, God works with us as keepers of the vineyard, bringing our children to ripeness in Him.

Fruit can provide spiritual illustrations for our children. Since the orange can be divided into segments, it's a reminder to share the message of Jesus with others. Children know about the apple in the garden. They might like to know that Christmas trees were once decorated with apples, honoring Jesus, the last Adam, who reversed the curse of the Fall (I Corinthians 15:45).

Moment With My Child:

Does fruit grow on trees or on vines? That was a tricky question. They grow on both!

Jesus told a story about a vine and its branches. Jesus is the vine, and we are the branches, growing out from Him. When we keep our hearts connected to Him, we can grow the fruit of loving Him and others. We stay connected by reading the Bible, talking to God, and praising Him. Every time we're with Jesus, it's like He gives us "food" and "water" to help us grow. People can learn about Jesus when they see His fruit in our lives.

I am the vine, you are the branches; he who abides in Me…bears much fruit. John 15:5

BRANCH

FRUIT

VINE

December 13: Shepherds in the Fields

Shepherds were watching their sheep by night, on high alert against nighttime predators. They were constantly committed to the sheep in their care. When we were expecting our first child, someone said to me, "Enjoy your maiden sleep." It was only after the baby arrived that I truly understood those words. A mother is forever "plugged in" to her child, hearing its every cry. In that respect, shepherds and mothers are a lot alike. Both are on perpetual night call.

Psalm 23 summarizes the care of Jesus for us, His sheep. He provides rest and sustenance, in green pastures and by still waters. When we near danger, He pulls us in with His crook. With His rod He fends off Satan. When we are downcast, He restores our soul.

In the Luke 15 parable of the lost sheep, Jesus says that if we get lost, He will leave the other ninety-nine of the flock to find and rescue us. In John 10, Jesus lovingly describes His role as the Good Shepherd. He is the one Who guards us and calls us by name. We recognize His voice, and we follow Him.

Jesus understands our hearts as mothers. Isaiah 40:11 says that He tends His flock like a shepherd, gathering the lambs in His arms and carrying them close to His heart. Likewise, He gently leads those with young. Jesus leads us, as we point our children to their Shepherd.

Moment With My Child:

Shepherds were the first to hear that Jesus had been born. The people didn't think that shepherds were important, but God did. They were like Jesus, the Good Shepherd. When lambs were born, the shepherds wrapped them in swaddling clothes and laid them in a manger to keep them from being hurt. If the lambs were to be sacrifices in the temple, they had to be perfect in every way. Does that sound familiar? Jesus was also wrapped up and placed in a manger. One day Jesus would be the perfect Lamb for the sacrifice of the cross. Did you notice that Jesus is both a lamb and a shepherd? As our shepherd, He cares for us like a Mommy or Daddy, watching over us every day.

I am the good shepherd; I know my sheep and my sheep know me. John 10:14 NIV

December 14: Mistletoe

Moment For Mom:

For most of us, mistletoe represents the playful holiday practice of stealing a kiss from someone beneath its leaves and berries. But mistletoe carries with it a far more profound message, picturing the covenant relationship God has designed for His children. Mistletoe is a parasite. It can live only by burrowing deep into the tissue of a host tree. From the tree it draws the water and nutrients necessary for life. If it disconnects, it dies.

As God's children, we derive our love, power, and strength from Him. The truth is that God delights in being our host. From Him we draw our identity. He is the archer; we are His arrows. He is the writer; we are His story. He is our deliverer; we are His captives set free. We are who we are because we are anchored in Who He is. Our identity is secure, because He can never change.

In Ephesians, Paul advises us to send our roots deep into Christ, so that His love may dwell in our hearts by faith. That way, He can work through us according to His mighty power. If there's ever a time we need to be rooted in Christ's love, it's at Christmas, as a frantic shopper "steals" our parking place, or an unexpected "must-do" invades our calendar, or that difficult person steps on our very last nerve. Lord, please keep us rooted in You.

Moment With My Child:

Mistletoe is a special type of plant called a parasite. When its seed lands on a tree, roots grow out and dig deep into the pulp of the tree. The mistletoe cannot live without the food and water it gets inside the tree. The Bible tells us to let our roots go deep into the love of Jesus. Do we have real roots on our bodies? Of course not! That would be silly. God is talking about roots we cannot see…the roots of our hearts. Our hearts can be very strong when they are rooted in Jesus. We take in His love and give it out to others. If we are wise we will be like the mistletoe, on its tree. We will cling to God every day.

Your roots will grow down into God's love and keep you strong. Ephesians 3:17 NLT

December 15: The Wise Men

Moment For Mom:

If shepherds were on the low rung of society, the wise men were near the top. Dressed in finery and bearing expensive gifts, the Magi followed the Numbers 24:17 star to the Christ Child. They came to worship, with gifts foreshadowing the coming life of the tiny babe.

GOLD is a gift befitting the King of Kings and the Lord of Lords.

FRANKINCENSE was a resin for temple worship, a pleasing fragrance in the nostrils of God. Jesus Himself would one day be the sacrifice, a pleasing aroma before His Father.

MYRRH was a burial spice, symbolizing Christ's death on the cross.

Just as the wise men followed a star, so we can follow Jesus, the "bright morning star" of Revelation 2:28. The morning star is the first one to appear each day, driving the darkness far away. Jesus gives us the light and direction that we need.

You may have heard the expression, "Wise men still seek Him." That's especially true for us mothers. We need His wisdom to train up our children in the individual ways which they should go (Proverbs 22:6). God tells us that if we lack wisdom, we are to ask Him for it (James 1:5).

Lord, help each of us to be that Proverbs 31:2 woman, with wisdom on her tongue and in her instruction. May we point our children to the Morning Star, that He may lead them.

Moment With My Child:

Do you know what wisdom means? It means seeing things from God's point of view. It means thinking like God thinks. Now, how do we do that? We learn God's thoughts from the stories of the Bible and from listening to what God says. The wise men followed the star that they had heard about in Scripture. That's what made them wise.

When the wise men came, they brought gifts to the Christ Child. One of the gifts was gold, which is very expensive. Just think. We can give Him a gift more valuable than gold. We can give Him our hearts.

We saw His star in the east and have come to worship Him. Matthew 2:2

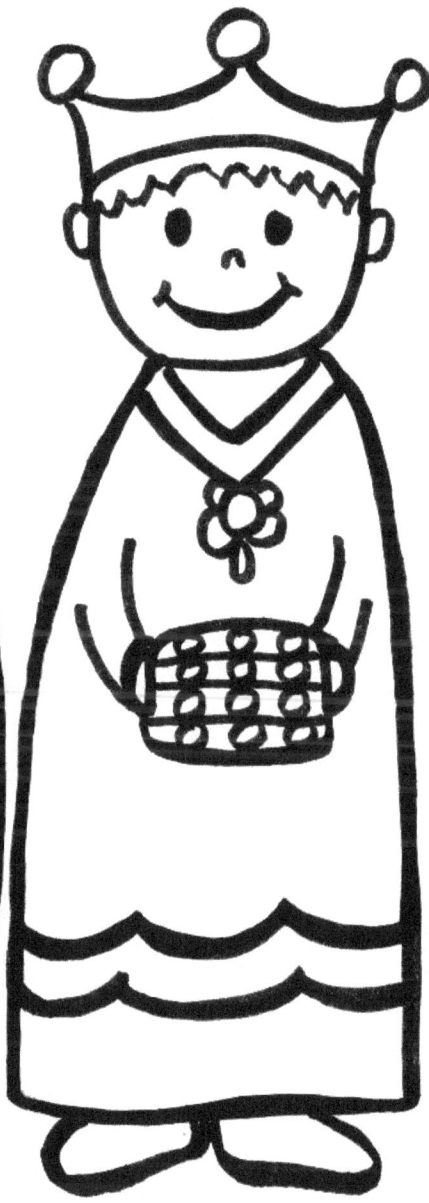

December 16: Christmas Music

Moment For Mom:

For twenty-four days Frederick Handel sequestered himself while writing his *Messiah*. When he emerged from his marathon, he declared that he had seen both the majesty of heaven and "the great God Himself." The result was the celestial music which brought King George II to his feet for its Hallelujah Chorus. Filled with the glory of Jesus, our reigning king, Handel's music speaks the universal language of the heart. It lifts us before God's throne of grace.

Not as majestic, but just as profound, are the Christmas carols we sing. Steeped in sound theology, they proclaim the mystery of Christ's coming. Take, for example, the second verse of "Hark the Herald Angels Sing." It's the mystery of the Incarnation and man's salvation, all in one verse:

Mild He lays His glory by, born that man no more may die.
Born to raise the sons of earth, born to give them second birth.

Scripture calls both voices and musical instruments to praise God. But recently I was reminded of another instrument: our hearts. One old hymn implores God, "Tune my heart to sing Thy praise." Not long ago, one of my granddaughters was visiting and heard her daddy whistling downstairs. When she could not determine the source of the melody, she beamed at me, "Nana, your heart is singing!" We might call that the naiveté of a child, but I believe there was wisdom beyond her years. Whether we realize it or not, our hearts can sing a joyful tune or a mournful dirge, depending on our attitude. Lord, give me a heart at Christmas that sings of Your praise, not of the items on my to-do list. Let my life be a song to Your glory.

Moment With My Child:

Christmas carols tell us about the very first Christmas. "Away in a Manger" and "O Little Town of Bethlehem" tell us about where Jesus was born. Psalm 8:2 says that the singing of children is very special to God. He loves to hear you sing about His Son. What is your favorite Christmas carol? Would you like to sing it now?

Oh, come let us sing with joy to the Lord. Psalm 95:1

December 17: Angels

Moment For Mom:

It would be hard to imagine the Christmas story without angels. First there was Gabriel, who announced to Mary that God had chosen her to be the mother of His Son. Then came the angel who assured Joseph that Mary's story about the pregnancy was true; he should take her as his wife. Finally came the angels who proclaimed to the shepherds the divine birth. Angels are, in effect, God's messengers. Psalm 103:20 says that angels are "mighty ones who carry out his plans, listening for each of his commands" (NLT). They do His will.

God uses humans as His messengers, too. He has committed the gospel to us and in His great commission (Matthew 28:16-20), He commands us to carry it to all the world.

As mothers, we are messengers to our children. Deuteronomy 6:8 tells us to take God's commands and "impress them on your children. Talk about them when you sit at home and when you walk along the road, when you lie down and when you get up." In God's eyes, being His messenger to our children is a very important job.

In a real sense, God has ordained mothers as human mirrors, reflecting to their children the gifts and temperaments that God has given them. I can remember saying to my children, "Look how compassionate you were. I'll bet God will use you to care for others." Or, "look at those colors you chose. God made you very artistic." To be God's conduits, we need to listen to Him as the angels do. God, help me hear your desires for my children and to guide them along the way.

Moment With My Child:

Do you remember how the shepherds felt when they saw an angel? Yes, that's right. They were very surprised and also a little afraid. That's because the angel was very bright and shiny. It carried the glory of God. Angels are God's very special messengers. He has made us His messengers, too. We can tell our friends about why Jesus came to earth. We can tell them that Jesus died for our sins. We can carry good tidings of great joy, just like the angels.

Send us around the world with the news. Psalm 62:2 TLB

December 18: Pine Cones

Moment For Mom:

There's just something about a pine cone that begs to be glued and glittered. But the pine cone's enticing texture is not its only reason for being. Underneath its scales are seeds, and seeds are at the heart of the Christmas message. As early as Genesis 3, when Adam and Eve fell, God promised that the seed of a woman would retaliate against Satan. Jesus was both the seed of a woman and through the power of the Holy Spirit, the seed of God.

In John 12, Jesus says that like a seed, He must fall to the ground and die, to bring forth life. This He did on the cross. As we are born again in Christ, we repeat the dying process, becoming dead to sin and alive to God. We are re-born, "not of perishable seed, but of imperishable, that is, through the living and abiding word of God" (I Peter 1:23).

God gave us both His living seed, Jesus, and His written seed, the Bible (Luke 8:11). God, as planter, cultivates the seeds of His word in our hearts. As mothers, we plant the seeds of the word in our children, as we read them the Bible and teach them verses. As we do so, we are raising up trees of righteousness in God's kingdom.

Pine cones from nature find their festive way into our decorations. But just think. We can be living pine cones, carrying in our words and actions the seeds of God's good news.

Moment With My Child:

Have you ever planted a seed in a plastic container to watch it grow? What happens? First the seed splits apart. Then roots go down in the soil. Finally the new plant shoots upward, from the top of the seed. It's like that with the seeds of a pine cone. When the cone falls to the ground, the seeds land on the soil and begin to grow. Before you know it, new little pine trees are on their way. In the Bible, Jesus is called the Seed. When we ask Him into our hearts, new life begins to grow in us. The Bible is also called God's seed. As we read the Bible, it's like planting more and more seeds in our heart. We become more and more like Jesus.

I have hidden your word in my heart. Ps. 119:11 NLT

December 19: The Christmas Feast

Moment For Mom:

When Christmas dinner comes near, out pop the favorite family recipes, sacred for generations. You can count on Granny's award-winning sweet potatoes and Aunt Jane's famous corn pudding. The "good" plates come out of the cupboard, a centerpiece decorates the table, and the buffet holds enough food to feed a small army. All in all, it's a feast for a king. And that's how it should be. The rich feast that we spread signifies the rich treasure God gave us in His Son. We can invite Jesus as the guest of honor (Revelation 3:20).

When we gather for Christmas dinner, it points to another feast that we can one day enjoy in heaven. That celebration is called the wedding feast of the Lamb. Jesus, the Sacrificial Lamb, is the groom at the feast, and we, the church, are His bride. Those attending the feast must wear a white robe. It's an invisible garment of righteousness, given to everyone cleansed in the Savior's blood.

Moment With My Child:

What's your favorite part of Christmas dinner? Turkey? Mashed potatoes? Buttered rolls? Yum! There are so many good things to eat, especially the desserts. But our Christmas feast is not nearly as wonderful as the feast that God has prepared in heaven for those who love Him. We cannot even imagine how wonderful it will be. Jesus will be there. So will all those who have asked Jesus to live in their hearts. To attend the feast, you must be wearing a white robe. We can't see it, but God can. It's called a robe of righteousness, which means having all our sins taken away. We can't go to the store and buy the white robe. Only Jesus could buy it for us, through His death on the cross. We can have His perfectly white record, just by asking for it. Do you wonder what the feast of the Lamb will be like? So do I. It will be a special surprise.

The wedding feast is ready. Matthew 22:8, NLT

Mom note: When you color your plate for the feast, add any food to it that you'd like to draw.

December 20: Christmas Candles

One Christmas Eve our neighborhood lined our streets and walkways with hundreds of luminaries. For months we had collected plastic milk jugs, then secured candles in them with sand. Now it was time to light the candles, welcoming Christ into our hearts and homes.

A candle in a window has long been the sign of welcome for weary travelers. It is a sign for Jesus, as He arrives on His journey from heaven to earth. The flame suggests the burning love of the Father in sending Jesus: "For God so loved the world that He gave His only begotten Son, that whoever believes in Him shall not perish, but have eternal life" (John 3:16).

As mothers, we can light welcome candles for our children. It's an unwritten sign that says, "My heart is always open for you." I saw this modeled at a ballet rehearsal, years ago, when everything was going wrong. At the height of the turmoil, a tutu'ed cherub approached the director and tugged on her skirt. I watched the director's face as a quick, fervent prayer slipped heavenward. Then she dropped everything and squatted to the little one's level. "What is it, Honey?" she calmly questioned. The child was oblivious to what that moment had cost the director. But it set an indelible goal for me as a mother. Lord, help me put God's love on a candlestick in all the dailies of life (Matthew 5:15). Let a candle always burn in my open heart.

Moment With My Child:

Long ago, people put candles in their windows to let others know that they were welcome. At some churches, people hold candles on Christmas Eve as a sign that Jesus is welcome. Jesus told his followers to take His light and be like candles for others. He told them not to hide their light, but to put it on a candlestick, for all to see. We can light the darkness of those who don't know Jesus. As He comes into our hearts, He lights a candle that shines within us. It's not a real candle. But its glow is real, when others see us loving and obeying Him. How can you light a welcome candle for Jesus, by how you love and obey?

Let your light shine before men. Matthew 5:16

December 21: Christmas Stockings

Moment For Mom:

All year long I look for stocking stuffers to surprise my family at Christmas. Since the third century people have been hanging stockings, largely because of the legend of St. Nicholas. Nicholas was a Turkish bishop who loved to help the poor. One day he heard about a man whose daughters could not marry, because they had no dowries. Somehow Nicholas managed to slip gold coins in the girls' stockings, which they had washed and hung over the fireplace to dry. Today, people hang stockings in their own homes, in hopes of receiving a blessing.

In a similar vein, but to a greater extent, God fills the "stockings" of our lives from the storehouse of His blessings. He knows what we need, even before we ask Him. Some needs are physical, like food, shelter, and clothing. Others are intangible, like love, joy and peace.

This spring, a bird built her nest in our yard. After the eggs hatched, the nestlings stretched their mouths wide, expecting to be fed. It reminded me of Father God, Who fills our lives with good things. "Open your mouth wide," says God. "I will fill it" (Psalm 81:10). Christmas is a time to consider the goodness of God. Sometimes Christmas can stir up past grief or unhappy memories. Rehearsing God's faithful blessings can bring the soothing Balm of Gilead (Jeremiah 8:22) to that pain.

Moment With My Child:

What do you like to get in your stocking? Candy? Gum? Toys? I like to be surprised just like you! Have you ever wondered why we hang stockings in our homes? It's because of "Good Ole St. Nick." Long ago, there was a bishop named Nicholas who loved to help people in need. One day he heard about three sisters who could not marry because their father did not have money for the groom's gift. Nicholas managed to drop gold coins into stockings which the young girls had washed and put over the fireplace to dry. Everyone was overjoyed. God is like St. Nick, always putting gifts into our lives. He gives us our family, friends, yummy food, warm beds, and oh so many things. What has God given you?

Whatever is good and perfect comes down to us from God our Father. James 1:17 NLT

Mom Note: Would you like to put your name on this stocking?

December 22: Nativity Scene

Moment For Mom:

As an infant, my brother played Jesus in a nativity scene. He didn't cry, but he did tickle Mary's nose with the straw. She forgave him, and God didn't mind. We were celebrating His Son.

Many of us place nativity scenes in our homes. Children love to play with the characters before Christmas, then put the Christ Child in the manger on Christmas Eve. In the scene are the highest and lowest of society, from the ragged shepherds, who were considered ritually unclean, to the wise men, well-educated and richly dressed. Everyone is welcome to bow before the King. Because of Jesus, we can "draw near with confidence to the throne of grace, so that we may receive mercy and find grace to help in time of need" (Hebrews 4:16). Grace is God's unmerited favor, meant for all mankind. Regardless of what we have done, God will receive a repentant soul.

The spectrum of humanity at the nativity scene is a preview of what we can expect in heaven. There we will see a multitude "out of every nation and all tribes and people and tongues, standing before the throne and before the Lamb" (Revelation 7:9). God says that He does not want anyone to perish, but for all to come to repentance (II Peter 3:9).

Moment With My Child:

Who do we usually see in nativity scenes? That's right! (*Mary and Joseph, the shepherds, wise men, angels, animals, and of course, Baby Jesus.*) Baby Jesus is the most important one of all. God Himself came to earth as a tiny baby. What do you notice about the shepherds and the wise men? They look very different. The shepherds are poor and dirty. Their clothes are ragged and plain. The wise men are rich and powerful. You can see that because their clothes are fancy, and their gifts for Jesus cost a lot of money. It doesn't matter to God if you are rich or poor. Everyone can worship Jesus. Will God stop loving us if we do something really bad? No! When we tell God we're sorry, He is always ready to forgive us. We can always come before Him.

Turn to Me and be saved, all the ends of the earth. Isaiah 45:22

December 23: Christmas Lights

Moment For Mom:

Think Clark Griswold. Think *Christmas Vacation*! Think CHRISTMAS LIGHTS! When I was a child, our favorite Christmas activity was piling in the family car—which looked like a cumulus cloud on wheels—then searching for lights of Griswold proportions. Not much has changed. Lights are the flagship of Christmas. That's appropriate, because Jesus calls Himself the light of the world (John 8:12).

The coming of the Messiah was prophesied in terms of the light that He would bring. "The people dwelling in darkness have seen a great light, and on those dwelling in the region and shadow of death, on them a light has dawned" (Matthew 4:16 ESV). Before coming to Jesus, we "were once darkness," but now we "are light in the Lord. Live as children of light" (Ephesians 5:8 NIV). When a light switches on, darkness must flee.

The light of God can be bright, like when He quickens our understanding. Or it can be a soft light, reminding us of His presence. His word is a lamp to our feet and a light to our path (Psalm 119:105). With it He guides us, so that we can guide our children. Lord, let my words and actions light the path for others, especially my children, to come to You.

Moment With My Child:

Do you like colorful lights or bright, white ones? I like them both. They are really shiny. During Christmas, we see them everywhere: on houses and trees, and even at the mall. Christmas lights can remind us of Jesus, because he is the light of the world. The brightness of Jesus can be like a flashlight, showing us the path to follow. Or sometimes He's like the glowing night light in your room, making you feel safe. The Bible is called a light for your feet, keeping you from stumbling. Jesus says that you can be a light in the world, too. As you tell others about Jesus, you light the way to Him. As you obey Him, others will see how to walk in His way.

I am the light of the World. John 8:12

December 24: The Babe in the Manger

Moment For Mom:

"Away in a manger, no crib for a bed, the Little Lord Jesus lay down His sweet head."

Jesus called Himself the bread of life. It's no wonder, then, that the Christ Child was placed in a manger, a feeding trough for animals. In French, the word "manger" means "to eat." Jesus calls us to eat of Him, the living bread. We are to draw our spiritual life from Him (Numbers 11:6-9).

The manna in the desert prefigured the coming of Jesus. It sustained the people, dropping each day from heaven, to save them from death. Jesus spoke of Himself in the same terms: "It is My Father who gives you the true bread out of heaven. For the bread of God is that which comes down out of heaven, and gives life to the world" (John 6:32-33). Jesus came down out of heaven, taking on human likeness (Philippians 2:7).

We can "eat" of the finished work of Jesus to avoid spiritual death. "Everyone who beholds the Son and believes in Him will have eternal life" (John 6:40). We can also "eat" of God's word, for "man does not live on bread alone but on every word that comes out of the mouth of God" (Matthew 4:4 NIV). Lord, I choose to be nourished by Your word, that I might have spiritual bread to feed my children. You are my eternal and my daily bread. Because of You, I will never go hungry (John 6:35).

Moment With My Child:

When Jesus was born, He was placed in a manger. A manger is a wooden stand where animals come to eat. Look at this picture of Baby Jesus. He is snuggled on a soft bed of hay. Hay is what animals eat when their tummies get rumbly. What happens when *your* tummy gets rumbly? That's right! You get a snack. Sometimes our hearts need a snack, too. They might feel rumbly because they are sad, angry or afraid. What do we do then? It's time to go to the Bible for a snack. Oh, we don't really eat the pages of the Bible. But we listen to what God has to say. He made us, and He knows how we feel. A good snack from His word makes our hearts strong, all over again.

**Man shall not live by bread alone, but by every word that comes
from the mouth of God. Matthew 4:4 ESV**

December 25: Gift Giving

Moment For Mom:

In the movie *The Christmas Story*, young Ralphie cringes as he models the pink bunny suit Aunt Clara made for him. He said it was not a surprising gift from one who always saw him as "a four-year-old girl." Who started this gift thing, anyway? Interesting question. Maybe it's because the Magi brought gifts. And certainly it shows our love for others. I like to think we are honoring the very first Christmas gift: Jesus Himself. He was God's "gift too wonderful for words" (II Corinthians 9:15 NLT). God, our creator, is not at all like Aunt Clara. He knows us through and through, and so He gave us a Savior. Jesus alone can bring us the eternal life for which we yearn. He is our ultimate fulfillment, on earth and forever.

Sadly, many people give Christmas gifts, year after year, without receiving God's greatest gift, Jesus. For twenty-nine years, I was among them. I thought it was up to me to accumulate good works, so I could buy my ticket to heaven. The truth was that long ago, Jesus purchased eternal life for me by dying on the cross. I simply needed to confess my sins and ask Jesus to take control of my life. Finally I understood that I could be saved solely by God's grace, His unmerited favor. It was not by my works, but a free gift from God (Ephesians 2:8-9).

Moment With My Child:

Have you ever saved up your money to buy a gift for someone? Maybe it was a gift they could not afford themselves. Well, that's what Jesus did for us, when He died on the cross. He bought us a gift we could never pay for ourselves. He bought us the gift of heaven. When Jesus lived, He never, ever sinned. He had a perfect score in life. Do you know anyone, besides Jesus, who has never sinned? No, neither do I. By asking Jesus into our hearts, we get His perfect score as our own. His score is our ticket into heaven one day. What a gift! Let me ask you this: do we pay for gifts people give us? No. Then it would not be a gift. Jesus paid the full price for the best gift ever: a chance to be with Him in heaven.

God saved you by his grace when you believed….it is a gift from God.

Ephesians 2:8 NLT

December 26: Love, the Heart of the Season

MOMENT FOR MOM:

Can you even imagine sending your child to death, to pay for someone else's crime? I can't either. Sometimes, when I mess up big time, I think, "If I were Jesus, I wouldn't have died for me." But God's love is not limited, like ours is. Try to get your mind around this one: John 17:26 says that as we receive Jesus, God pours into us the same love He has for His Son. That's right! God loves us the same way He loves Jesus. Amazing thought!

The love we extend to God and others initiates from Him. "We love because He first loved us" (I John 4:19). Once again we are totally dependent on God. First He gave us the great commandments, to love Him and others well. Then He enabled us to fulfill those very commandments. "Those who are loved by God, let his love continually pour from you to one another, because God is love" (I John 4:7 TPT).

The picture of God continually filling our love tanks is a good one for mothers. We are constantly pouring affection and attention on our children. It doesn't take long for us to feel like we are running on fumes. When we feel like we have overdrawn our love-accounts, it's a good time to ask God for a fresh deposit. Remember, His mercies are new every morning (Lamentations 3:22-23). Of course, you can ask between mornings too! God's love never runs dry. For our love to be a continuous stream, it needs to flow from Him, our source

MOMENT WITH MY CHILD:

You know how you feel when you love someone? Well, that's the way God feels when He thinks about you. His love for you is as deep as the ocean and as high as the sky. How big is that? Yes! God's love is HUGE! As God pours His love into our hearts, He gives us the power to love Him back and to love those around us. I'll bet you have filled a cup with water before. Well, that's what God does for us. He fills our hearts with love, over and over again.

We love because He first loved us. I John 4:19

www.ingramcontent.com/pod-product-compliance
Lightning Source LLC
Chambersburg PA
CBHW081546040426
42448CB00015B/3239